Taguchi

Fantasy on Ice
❦— 2023 —❦
OFFICIAL PHOTO BOOK
MAKUHARI / MIYAGI / NIIGATA / KOBE

Fantasy on Ice 2023

MAKUHARI
2023.5.26-5.28
幕張イベントホール

MIYAGI
2023.6.2-6.4
セキスイハイムスーパーアリーナ

YUZURU HANYU
羽生結弦

N.Tanaka

Y.Taguchi

N.Tanak

y on Ice

Y.Taguchi

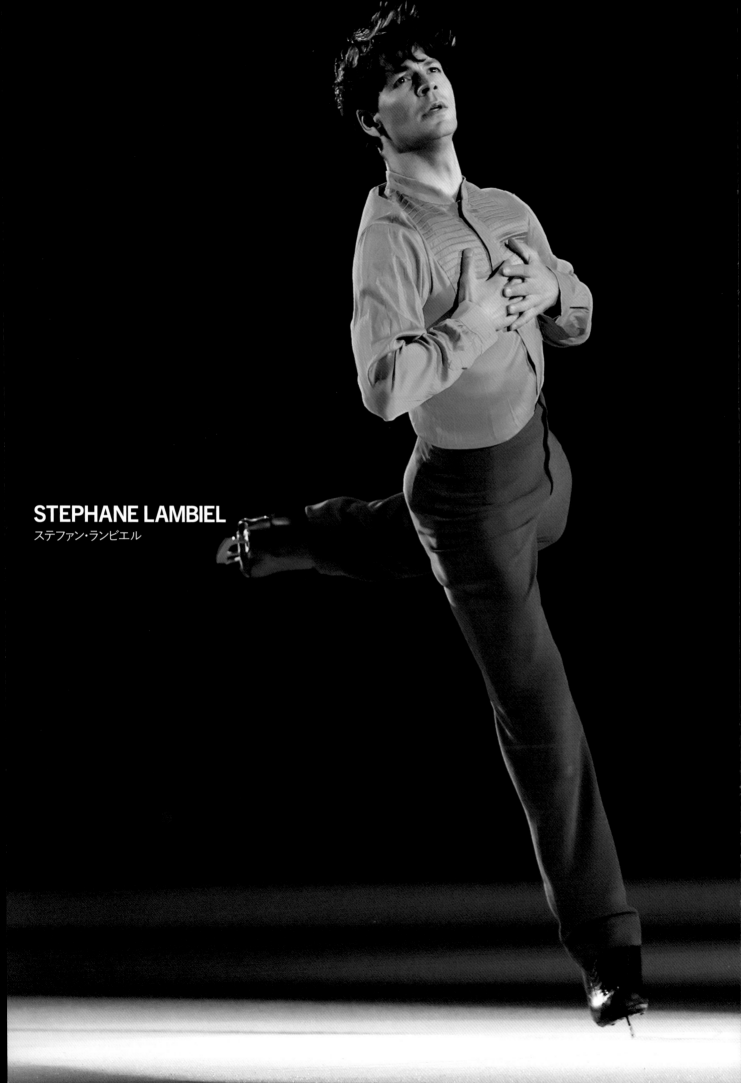

STEPHANE LAMBIEL

ステファン・ランビエル

JAVIER FERNANDEZ
ハビエル・フェルナンデス

N.Tanaka

N.Tanak

N.Tanaka

JOHNNY WEIR
ジョニー・ウィア

S.Noto

SHIZUKA ARAKAWA
荒川静香

Y.Taguchi

N.Tanaka

NOBUNARI ODA

織田信成

S.Noto

Y.Taguchi

KEIJI TANAKA
田中刑事

N.Tanaka

SOTA YAMAMOTO
山本草太

Taguchi

S.Noto

KAZUKI TOMONO
友野一希

S.Noto

MAI MIHARA
三原舞依

.Noto

GABRIELLA PAPADAKIS &
GUILLAUME CIZERON
ガブリエラ・パパダキス＆
ギヨーム・シゼロン

N.Tanaka

S.Noto

LILAH FEAR &
LEWIS GIBSON

ライラ・フィアー＆
ルイス・ギブソン

S.Noto

Fantasy on Ice

Y.Taguchi

**MERY ACEVEDO &
ALFONSO CAMPA**
メリー・アセベド＆
アルフォンソ・カンパ

AERIAL
AiRY JAPAN
増保衣里子、檜山宏子、板津由佳
BLUE TOKYO
新井智貴、有木真太郎、大舌恭平

Y.Taguchi

Fantasy on 'Ice

ENSEMBLE SKATERS
アンサンブルスケーターズ

Fantasy on Ice 2023

NIIGATA
2023.6.16-6.18
朱鷺メッセ

KOBE
2023.6.23-6.25
神戸ワールド記念ホール

M.Takahashi

Fantasy on Ice

S.Noto

YUZURU HANYU

羽生結弦

N.Tanaka

S.Noto

S.Noto

S.Not

M.Takahashi

N.Tanaka

S.Noto

N.Tanaka

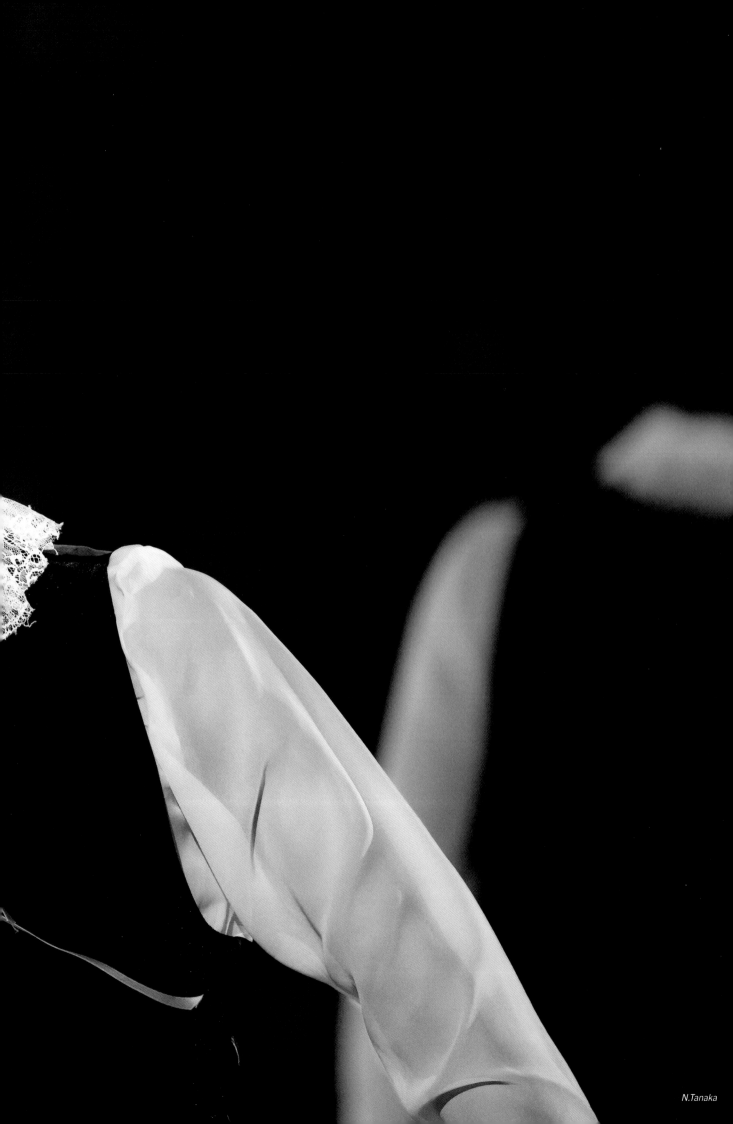

N.Tanaka

S.Noto

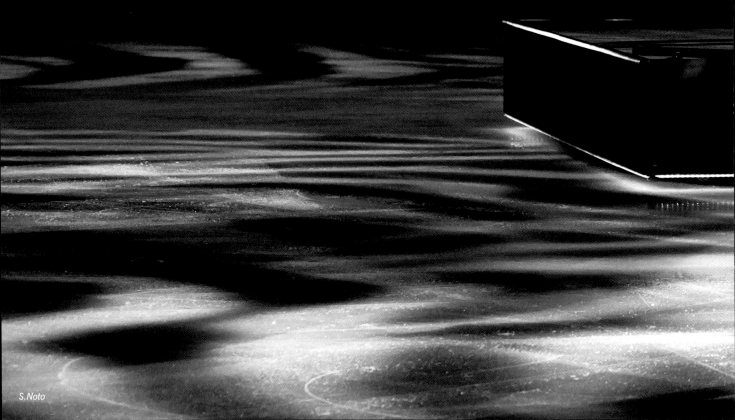

S.Noto

STEPHANE LAMBIEL
ステファン・ランビエル

N.Tanaka

JAVIER FERNANDEZ
ハビエル・フェルナンデス

N.Tanaka

S.Noto

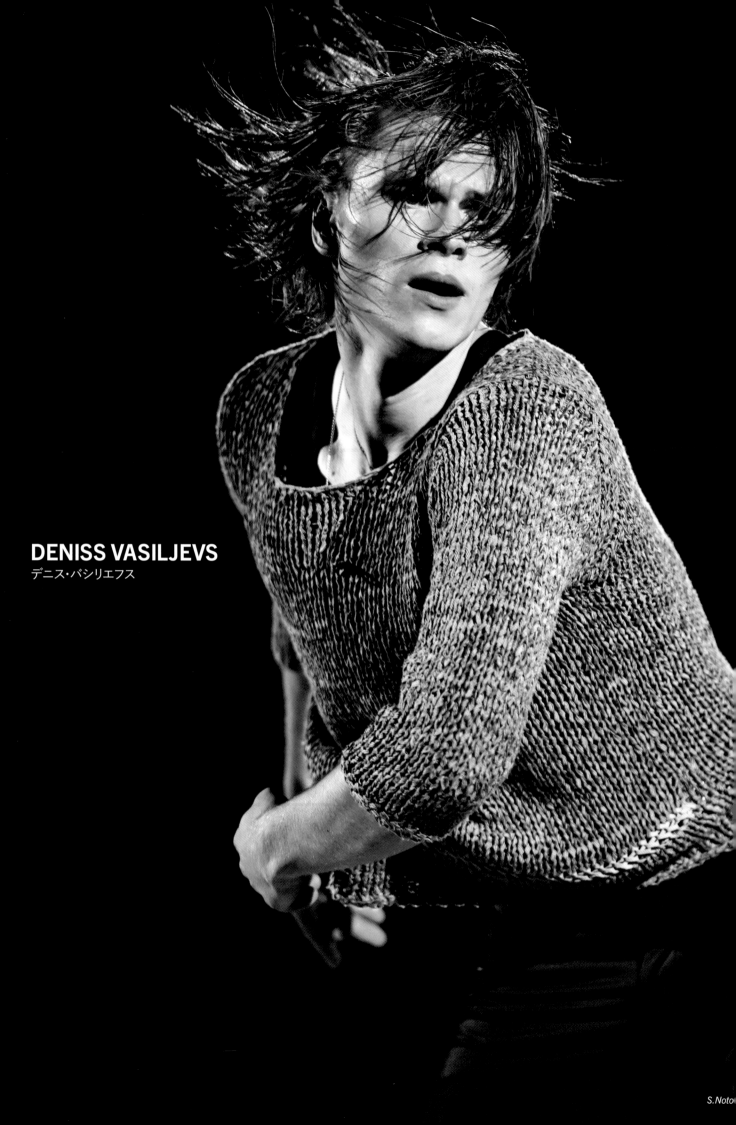

DENISS VASILJEVS
デニス・バシリエフス

S.Noto

S.Noto

NOBUNARI ODA
織田信成

S.Note

.Takahashi

KEIJI TANAKA
田中刑事

S.No

KAORI SAKAMOTO
坂本花織

M.Takahas.

SATOKO MIYAHARA

宮原知子

M.Takahashi

N.Tanak

TAKAHITO MURA

無良崇人

M.Takahas

S.Noto

MAI MIHARA
三原舞依

N.Tanaka

M.Takahashi

N.Tanaka

**GABRIELLA PAPADAKIS &
GUILLAUME CIZERON**

ガブリエラ・パパダキス＆
ギヨーム・シゼロン

N.Tanaka

S.Noto

**PIPER GILLES &
PAUL POIRIER**
パイパー・ギレス＆
ポール・ポワリエ

N.Tanaka

N.Tanaka

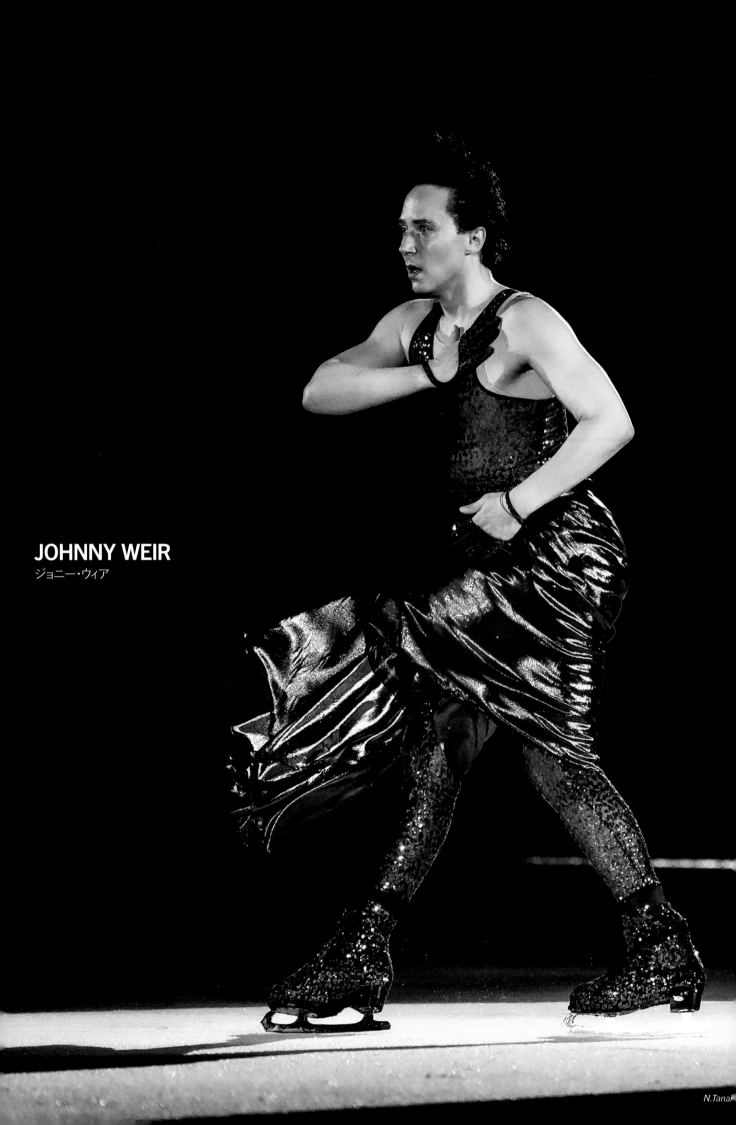

JOHNNY WEIR
ジョニー・ウィア

N.Tana

N.Tanaka

M.Takahash

S.Noto

S.Noto

N.Tanaka

Fantasy on I...

M.Takahashi

KIMI
（DA PUMP）

ISSA
（DA PUMP）

RIMI NATSUKAWA
夏川りみ

MIHO FUKUHARA
福原みほ

MIKA NAKASHIMA
中島美嘉

DEAN FUJIOKA
ディーン・フジオカ

TOUYA KOBAYASHI
小林柊矢

FANTASY ON ICE SPECIAL BAND

CHOREOGRAPHER

鳥山雄司
音楽監督／Guitar

NAOTO
Violin

宮崎裕介
Keyboard

デイビッド・ウイルソン
振付

宮本賢二
振付